The Region's Violence

for Amy + Mark
with all good wishes
from
Ruth .

___

Nashville,
February 1985

RUTH FAINLIGHT

The Region's Violence

HUTCHINSON OF LONDON

HUTCHINSON & CO (*Publishers*) LTD
3 Fitzroy Square, London W1

London Melbourne Sydney
Auckland Johannesburg Cape Town
and agencies throughout the world

First published 1973

*This book has been set in Bembo type, printed in Great Britain
on antique wove paper by Benham and Company Limited, of Colchester,
Essex, and bound by Wm. Brendon, of Tiptree, Essex*

ISBN 0 09 115361 1

Some of these poems have been published in:

Antaeus
Mediterranean Review
The New Yorker
New York Times
The Poetry Review
The Scotsman
Southern Review, University of Louisiana
Sunday Times
Works In Progress
Poetry (Chicago)
European Judaism
Twentieth Century

Poems

The Dolphins

No day, no night,
Tides drift me here from somewhere else.
I find myself at my desk
Or the kitchen, in bed in the darkness.
What time is it, where have I come from,
Why am I returning?

No connection
Between these surfacings.
Like two dolphins twisting silently
In deep water, my thoughts grapple.
They separate to breathe, then plunge
Back into battle.

Out of the taut shield
Of underbelly, suave curve shaped
By three pressures: water, intestine, muscle—
His pale penis, unfurled
Into its own dimension, flaunts
The freedom of a blossom.

Her belly tapers to a faint cleft,
Dimple of generation—which must gape wide
In birth, when clouds of blood
Disperse through water—
A flower, a torn poppy
With falling petals.

Smooth and broad as a baby's battering ram
Of skull, the bulge of their heads.
And the same bland eyes, amused
Perhaps through accident of folds—
Yet so ironic. In love
Their eyes are closed.

Language exists, but
I cannot understand the dolphin's language.
What do they say as they couple?
Below the water's demarcation line
Conflict is muffled. But questions rise
In swathes of air-bubbles.

They cannot survive
In either element alone, unmixed.
Their love is enacted between breaths,
Between leaps, in mid-ocean depths—
Where every contact jolts
All explanations.

Time's Passing

Time's passing means that statements made,
(Written), as if / dictated by
The oracle who is oneself
At last come clear. Nothing is added.

Every factor there since that
Moment when the pattern set,
When all stars stood still/
Focussed their beams upon your perfect head
Confirming your identity/
Were in conjunction.

Whatever followed was indeed
Only necessity for action/
(Time a fickle ally),—skill
To prise the mask free from your face.

When that tide shrugs away, retreats,
And clouds move slow and inexorable
Across your special constellation,
It will be too late. The scroll
Will be snapped-to and filed. (Among
So many stars, how great the waste.)

God's Language

Angels have no memory,
God's language no grammar.
He speaks continually,
All words variations
Of his name, the world a web
Of names, each consonant
Proclaims a further meaning;
The unacceptable
Also the true, beyond
Time's bondage. Thus angels
Forget all contradictions,
Accepting every statement
As a commentary.
Their purpose is to gaze
Upon God's works, and listen,
Until the day that he
Pronounce the name: Messiah.

Tanya
(*Ché Guevara's last companion*)

How long did you lie hidden by the water's edge,
Nymph of corruption, brittle darkening lily,
Lips drawn back into the major grimace of death;
Nymph of ideology, still unperfected
Never to be imago of bright revolution,
With the frail elegance of a discarded chrysalis
In the rushes, a plundered mummy-case,
Or a disinterred sacrifice to Anubis—

As if old legends were true, and the body crumbles,
Detritus of a soul that wings to utopia
To soothe its frenzy for the unattainable—
Having been unsheathed by the one fated bullet
Whose searing metal entry metamorphized
Dream and desire and turmoil into rotting flesh.

Fire-Queen

Unseen, snow slides from over-laden boughs.
Spume of flakes, flurry of light, cold smoke;
Kaleidescope of crystal and lead and flame.
Then silence again as it sinks,
Weightless, lost, white into whiteness, down
To perma-frost encasing molten turbulence.

That core answers the sun-spots, flares
When her impotence most torments—she,
With her presumptions, her gestures, who has chosen
This place rather than any other
To expose herself to the gnawing ulcer
Of inertia, her own true nature.

Such is her kingdom—fire-queen
Of the absolute north, who rules by satire,
Inaction, disdain; touch blunted to ice,
Ears sealed, sight gone, reflection congealed, mirror
Shattered aeons ago, rather than see
Merely a pattern of line and colour, flat

As the diagram of what a face might be—
Which to recognise would mean to accept
That clamour of voices, imploring, complaining,
But silent, that rise from her brain like steam
From a tub-full of churning laundry.
But silent. Her thoughts—unspoken, ignored.

Their heat is the power that freezes, motor
Of her repression-machine, refrigerator
Of frightful patience, rigid mastodon throne,
Sealed and invisible ice-pyramid,
Red-hot iron-maiden of self-hatred
She's trapped inside by refusing to listen.

Screams settle like snow and never thaw.
Branches petrified under their burden
Of murdered desires. She sits like Lot's wife,
Beyond the need for praise or explanation,
Ambitionless as death, perfect, absorbed
Forever by her silent incantation.

Lilith

Lilith, Adam's first companion,
Assumed her equality.
For this she was banished.

God had created her
From the same earth as Adam.
She stood her ground, amazed
By the idea of differences.

Adam and God were embarrassed,
Humiliated. It was true—
They had been formed
At the same time, the two
Halves of His reflection.

Her expectations
Should have seemed justified.
But Adam needed to understand God.
A creature must now worship him,
Constrained and resentful
As he was. God encouraged him.

To guard His mystery, God
Caused Adam to swoon. There, when he awoke,
Awaited Eve, the chattel.

Eyes downcast, his phallus
The first thing she noticed.
The snake reminded her of it.
Easy to equate the two.

That nagging ache in his side
Where the rib was extracted
(In memory of which
The soldier thrust his spear)
Keeps Adam irritable.

Lilith's disgrace thus defined
Good and evil. She would be
Outside, the feared, the alien,
Hungry and dangerous.
His seed and Eve's fruit
At hazard from her rage.

Good wives make amulets
Against her, to protect themselves.
Lilith is jealous.

Silence

When you ask for consolation
From one of them, burnt children
Who were never loved—or so
The explanation runs—
They do not understand. Perhaps,
Like speech, it is a skill which must
Be learned at its specific
Moment. Once past, nothing
Yet known can activate
That latent aptitude.
The child remains both deaf and dumb;
The one you turned towards—
A loud, gesticulating mute.

How they torment, who always
Must retreat, as if attacked
By such demands, whose last defense
Becomes exposure of a pain
They moan and rage is fiercer far
Than yours. Heart-broken, you muffle
Your own complaint, adjusting to
The region's violence,
Leaving grief abused, unspoken—
Until, beyond the reefs
Of hopelessness, nothing seems lacking
In this solitude. You've grown
Accustomed to the silence.

snow poem

     birds stream over the houses opposite
I watch from my window
     one veers, passes through glass as if it were smoke
settles on my table

     it is snowing
     I stare at whirling flakes with such intensity
they drift into the room
transform it to a paper-weight

     all my flowers are dead
until the snow lies on them
revives their green and yellow
making them beautiful

     snow covers my papers
     the bird prints patterns with his feet
hieroglyphs appropriating
what I've written

     the bird flies up   one flake
approaches, huge, revealing
its precision and its symmetry
before it muffles me

My Hands

Even the most banal demand
From one with hands like mine
Asks too much. My palms seethe:
Blood so close beneath the skin
That plumps their sides, soft flesh incised
By stars and crescents under
Every finger, moon-creased at heel
Of thumb. I've wondered whether
One day I shall show stigmata.

Each palm's centre is a square
Of white. When I strain fingers back
The lines flush red like beading cuts—
A fate new-made each time I
Query it. Unless I deem them
Beautiful, my hands must seem
So violent, so timorous,
Stubborn and unreliable.
Therefore those who praise them win me.

My Eyes

A child, already I admired
Those eyes set deep in sockets, skin
Beneath stretched fine and dark and taut
Across the watched nerves' flicker, haughty
Arch of brow, and curve of hooded lid.

My eyes look like that now—accusing,
Mournful eyes which glare when I essay
A covert glance, eyes which betray
Because they neither show a hurt
Nor disguise curiosity.

But they can weep with such discretion
I forfeit sympathy—as if
I feared the taint of cowardice
More than other definition—insist
On staring-out whatever happens.

I use my eyes to guard and to repel.
I think I am invisible—
Except my eyes. My eyes are witnesses,
Calling the Perseus brave enough
To gaze unflinching at the basilisk.

Pigeons at Villa Belmonte

After he mounted her, wings fluttering
With joy of domination,
Neck iridescent with coppery
Lombardy green and the terra-
cotta of the Villa Belmonte;
(She smaller, darker, reserved—the same
Grey surrounding the shutters);
She strutted onto his neck, as if
In casual imitation; hopped off,
Then up and down, across, a few more times.
They bent their heads towards each other, seemed
Affectionate, their burbling cry conjugal.

I've read that pigeons, caged and left,
Will pluck each other bare and bleeding;
That they're more murderous
Than wolves, with no inborn restraint,
No code for peace which might allow
Retreat or dignified surrender.
Strange choice of symbol used
For love and tenderness, and yet,
Because they're beautiful, they serve.

Velasquez's 'Christ in the House of Martha and Mary'

You stare out of the picture, not at me.
Your sad, resentful gaze is fixed on what
I only see reflected in the mirror
On the wall behind your shoulder, perspective
Through an archway cut from sandy slabs of stone
The same warm brown from which you wove your bodice.
That old servant by your side is whispering
Admonitions and consolation—her
Country wisdom. But your attention lapses,
I believe, from those words of resignation
As much as from the pestle in your hand,
The plate of fish, white eggs and pewter spoon,
Wrinkled chilli and broken garlic cloves
Strewn across the table: this, your world,
Precise, material—all you yearn to leave,
Though fear and duty hold you. You cannot find
Courage for the negligence of faith
To justify a gesture similar—
And so what right to join your sister there?

Poetry

The poem, though derived from suffering, does
Not describe its chill of death.

As images intensify, they populate
Misery's absentness.

At first words will not come, in that hiatus
Anguish still is personal.

Then distance and disguise, the golden mask, retreat
Into expressiveness.

The Cripple's Mother

Maybe / I have ruined / my life:
The idea
        Seems self-indulgent, yet
Being so vulgar and
So satisfying,
It might be true.

A mother / loves
Her crippled child
With similar absorption:
Guilt
    Can eliminate
The need to think about
Anything else.

I guard this ruined life
From objectivity,
Cherish deformities
As they develop,
Make paper flowers
To decorate / the spectacle,
Attract attention.

When the maimed child dies,
Still hunched / behind his chair
She pushes it
                Along the pavement—
Blind to everything.
Her coat is shabby / her smile
Mystifying.

The Witch's Last Song

Lamb of Lucifer
So suave, so sulphur-white,
So strong. You hurt me
When you press into my womb,
Bite through my lips, obliterate
All air and light.
Oh, beautiful.
I arch beneath your weight
Become saintly
As I suffer
That same pain you felt
While hurtling down to Hell.
My sweat assuages your parched soul.
You drink my breath,
Revive with every groan
Wrung from me, each hot tear.
Milk rises in my breasts,
You suck them dry.
Still my sap exudes.
I can fly with you higher
Than the throne of Heaven,
Fall further than the deepest level
Of your kingdom,
Below sealed caves
Of minerals, and bones left by
The creatures before men.
We play together like two lambs,
God's lamb the third.
My lambs. One at each side.
My breasts could feed you both.
I shall be queen when I am burned.

Lake and Island

A lake is the opposite to an island.
Near the middle of the lake is an island.
Held between mountains, the lake seems an island.
A church stands alone on the island,
Roofless, a fountain of silence
That overflows its brim of time-worked stone,
Replenishes the lake and fruits the island.

Two Blue Dresses

What I should wear outweighs
Almost every speculation,
As if clothes could disguise.
A method to evade other
Uncertainties, and yet
The details of a costume
Re-collected serve to fix
The character of past events.

The era of that blue silk dress
Totally different from
The year I fell in love, revived
My aunt's old cashmere blue—
Its bias-cut and open-work,
That silver buckle-clasp
Low on the hip, enchanted me
Though out of fashion then,
The very fact became supporting.
I felt a heroine,
And just as well, those first weeks of
My first, unfortunate,
Short-lived affair. The stylish frock,
Eleventh birthday gift,
All ruched, had skirt and sleeves puffed out.
I can remember how
I stood and posed before the glass
Entranced, and half-afraid
To see reflected in my eyes
The probability
Of loneliness, but more, the wish
For all that came to pass.

I recognised the destiny
I still attempt to grasp.
I nerved myself to welcome it.

That moment, proud in finery,
Has seared my memory
More deeply than the tears I shed
In cashmere, in despair—
The end and the commencement of
My girlhood symbolised
By images as formalised
As rueful mannequins.

My Grandparents

Museums serve as my grandparents' house.
They are my heritage—but Europe's spoils,
Curios from furthest isles,
Barely compensate the fact
That all were dead before I was alive.

Through these high, dust-free halls, where
Temperature, humidity, access,
Are regulated, I walk at ease.
It is my family's house, and I
Safe and protected as a favoured child.

Variety does not exhaust me.
Each object witness to its own
Survival—the work endures beyond
Its history. Such proof supports me.
I do not tire of family treasures.

Because no-one remembers who they were,
Obscure existences of which I am
The only product, I merit
Exhibition here, the museum's prize,
Memorial to their legend.

Self-Conquest, Heroes and Dragons

Vain effort, when inspired by vanity,
Vain emulation, driven from such source,
Self-conquest can be easily defined:
Aggression's misdirected force—
Deception thrives on just this conflict.

Vanity and the desire to conquer it
Seep from the same chthonic spring:
Vanity and emulation, intertwined
Like sodden roots, almost block the exit.

False dreams, fear, and vanity:
In vain they are approached with violence.
Such stance implies the hero—dragons breed
Especially to flatter and delude him.

St. George may win the maiden, but gains
Nothing else. Meretricious symbol of
Self-conquest: the townsfolk clapping,
The painter ready at his easel.

Vain of his progress, a hermit wields his scourge
More single-mindedly. Thus vanity
Is banished, he consoles the bleeding flesh.
Every night dragons wrestle in his dreams.

Finally, vanity seems intrinsic.
Attempts to overcome it paralyse.
Vanity tells the truth regardless.
Confrontation is a vain manœuvre,
Side-stepping just another trap of pride.

The Climber

That light before the dawn,
Almost the light of negatives,
All grey, when everything
Shows clear and isolate,
So frail, so separate each twig
Each stone upon his path,
So lonely without colour yet.

The wind is strongest then,
Howls down the mountain side,
Is bitter cold. After the night,
The deepest tiredness assails
That climber who had thought
To reach the heights before
This moment of life's ebb.

Perhaps new day will never come.
Such light prefigures something else,
Another night behind
The distant peaks, or some
Further ordeal, demand,
Upon what strength he cannot feel
But hopes to find when called upon.

Disguise

She took the brush, began
To paint herself all black
The bristles dragged in streaks
Between the hairs
Along her arms.

She paddled paint
Over her breasts.
How that would frighten him
When he undid her dress.

Her cheeks were soon blacked out
One stroke across the brow
Another down her nose
The powder caked her lips
Thickened beneath her chin.
Its taste was bitter.

But she was painted out,
A ghost, a negative—
Released by this disguise
Into another world,
And safe from him;
From life; from death;
From everything.

The Betrothal

What is happening, why do they wrestle in the grass
Tearing aside the clothes that separate their skins?
If she wishes to defend herself, why
Do her limbs melt, why does she strain closer?
Even the earth beneath is more caressing than he.
Crumbling, it blots her cool from his sweat,
Its dryness soothes the chafe of their grinding.
And the rosebay-silk, whiteness unfurling
From split pods, confirms that love is precious.

And he, what is he doing? He's forgotten
Who she is. Something is pulling him down
To the earth's centre, there's an opening;
The grasses seem to be lashing his back,
Forcing him to push deeper and deeper.
Hair in his mouth and a voice distract.
The strength of this impulse to murder becomes
The fervent, whispered, phrase, 'I love you'.

Somewhere else love must be real, but not here.
This is beyond them both. They search
Each other's eyes, but only find themselves, minute,
Plunging through expanded pupils to nothing.
Each iris complicated as a stellar map,
Once embarked into that flecked immensity,
Distance and loneliness echo from the void
In answer to the question, 'Do you love me?'

The field is so deep, its soil a talc of bones.
He's far from her now, swinging between the planets,
But he's pressed her into, made her one with the earth.
She seeks comfort from all the dead who support her.
If she could hear them talk, perhaps they would explain
What love is—or perhaps the shadows of grass
And rosebay across his shoulder, like hieroglyphs,
Could be deciphered, if she will exchange
The rest of her life as payment for the answer.

Dreams

Hungry for dreams, I only have
To close my eyes, not even sleep,
And the dreams begin. Two people
Are talking, or I'm walking uphill
Through a sun-paled landscape. All day I'm tired.
By afternoon I cannot resist, I must lie down.

Then all attention strains,
Focussed upon the signal I dare not miss—
Images so banal I panic, and wake
And weep, and try to sleep again, plunge back
Into that pool where I'm swimming;
The room I saw once, as a child;
Faces from airports or bars
Which revealed so much more in a glance
Than through years of explaining.
I return to that high ridge of land—
Chalk soil and dusty grass—
Where I balanced, precarious
Between wrinkling waves and the cave-in
Which would plummet me beyond choice.

But the dreams insist: that other world
Whose irregular orbit carries it close
As a newly-captured moon,
Looming, foreboding in the sky,
Convulsing the surface below it.
All creatures of my planet
Cringe from its noisy death.

Oceans engulf cities
And driest peaks; and safe in my dream
I witness it all, more torn
By the moon's destruction than any danger.
But its metals have fused with the planet's core,
Seed found its destination.

I shall dream a new world if I can submit
To the pace of necessity:
Aeons to form the first cell, first man, myself—
Like a rose, a flag, the voice
To speak my message.

Isolates

Apart from present slights
And the more distant, larger,
Still effective hurts,

They brood about the bomb,
The planet's imminent destruction,
All human insignificance;

Those city isolates,
In parks, on benches;
Absorbed beyond awareness

Of the rain, and how it plasters
Thinning strands of hair
Against their vengeful temples.

Investigation of the Holy Woman

She lies all day in bed, for years
Has never moved out of the room.
They come to question her.
Dark-coated men with beards
Thrust fingers in her side,
White-coated ones attach their tubes
To analyse all bodily secretions,
Measure every ecstasy.
They listen to the voices speaking
Through her. Are these the words of God?
She will not eat.
The flesh of Jesus feeds sufficiently.
Pale limbs flung out, back arched
Into the martyr's bow, is she
Deluded or beatified?
Each Friday, wounds
Appear upon her brow and open
In the palm and instep. Odour
Of decay chokes each investigator
Before he enters, taints the corridor.
Her eyes roll upwards in that tranquil face
Varnished with blood like creosote.
She will not let them wipe the crust away—
Demands to be the scapegoat sacrificed
For blood to decorate the idol
She personifies
To all those others who
Leave alms and offerings and pray
Below her window in the muddy snow.

On the Moon

For those in thrall to the moon
Horizons are restricted—
Eye's evidence conflicts
With knowledge and reality.
Steep curvatures, abrupt appearances
And vanishings. Imagination
On the moon takes short breaths
But leaps higher. Shadows are absolute.
No nuance between black and white,
Dust so dry that anything dropped
Is lost forever, engulfed,
Without memorial,
And fluid tides swung round
A neighbouring, ambiguous planet.
Beneath the moon's surface
The entire past lies hidden. Its centre
A jumble of toys, tears, journeys,
Buried lovers and friends,
Its core a heart petrified.
Moon's day shifts slow across my brain,
From empty zone of fear to plenitude,
Cauterising its quarters,
Moving between two zeroes.

The Field

The field is trampled over utterly.
No hidden corner remains unchurned.
Unusable henceforth for pasture:
Sheep and cattle must feed elsewhere.

The field was torn by battle, dull
Explosions, trenches dug for shelter,
Vehicles which wheeled, reversed,
Hunted down the last resistance.

The field is strewn with bones and metal.
Earth which had not felt the air
During millenia, is now revealed
To every element and influence.

The undersoil surprises by its richness.
In battle's lull, at night, the farmer crawls
To estimate what might be salvaged
Of his lone field's potentiality.

If he survives, the field holds promise
Of great abundance, of a yield
To revolutionise his life.
The field is fertile. To survive is all.

The Ox

Yet still I tread the same straw
Deeper in the mud, still tethered
Must repeat the circle.
Monotony. But sullen rage
Does not abate, (gadflies torment
The ox), increases rather
As my feet grow heavy, clogged,
Their weight a penalty imposed
To make the task more irksome.

I want to build. Straw and mud
Should have become by now the bricks
I need in order to construct
The perfect city—(my sweat
Has baked them): vision which
I follow round the central post
And further down that awesome pit
The only monument as yet
My circling has created.

Bengal

They frighten me, those pictures
In the papers, things I read about,
The pictures which they make me see
Inside my head, exposures of deceit
And slaughter. Fear has corrupted me.
It's too revealing. Dull rage
That covers my retreat. Away, I cringe
Away, I seek the help of beauty.
That shocked face is Orpheus
With dead Eurydice cradled in his arms.
He staggers through mud, stunned, deaf
To the sound of guns or rain.
It's the same—God's punishment,
Or the cruelty which makes
Me compare their pain to art,
Attempt to alleviate
My impotence, ignore my cowardice.
She's beautiful, neck slack, glazed eyes.
My defense is this distancing.
But I see the faces I love
In place of hers; I identify,
Hopelessly; and fear is the worm
Who feeds on the corpse of beauty.

Build it Up, Tear it Down

Eliminate, scrape flesh from hide,
Splinter away the flakes of flint
That dull the blade. Or build it up
As patiently: sticks, stitches, stones,
The thousand cuts of an engraving.

Monotonous activity,
Like writing—repetition of
The same abstractions known as letters.
Even their shape is fascinating;
Patterns marked by pen on paper.

Silent boredom of gestation,
A trance of such intensity
As cells expand and multiply,
Elaborate primary structure
Through each inherent complication.

Implacable necessity
To recognise the truth that symbols
Come closest to reality.
When all else is eliminated
What remains must be essential.

Falling

I must let go, I must relax
My hands, dissolve my fear of falling.
My struggles overbalance me.

And should I fall, although no one
Would rescue me, no Anthony
With outstretched hand or cloak—

(The safety faith might guarantee,
The hope belief would give, along with
Punishment and category)—

The joy to have released my grip,
The stillness in that hurtling,
Might seem to last eternally.

Then

Unused and exhausted
By hours of silence
My body has stiffened
—Unmoving, inert in my chair,
Paralysed, convalescent—
A robot, an idol, a prisoner.
Then some circuit flickers, jarred
By introspection's boredom,
And memories stir, random, unconnected.

My mind becomes victim
Of a hazard profound and meaningless
As the encounter which produced me.
If the fusion of those cells can indicate
Intention, then whatever memory,
Partial as lightning, illuminates my brain,
Is neither more nor less significant.

Oh lovely sand, dun, sliding dry
Through my fingers, leaving a white powder,
Fine as flour, on my sun-browned skin.
Oh, bleached wood. I remember your greyness
Utterly now, grain harder and raised.
Beach-wood, desiccated, salt-encrusted.

Why do I see it so clearly? I crumbled a shell,
Looked vaguely around, then walked again.
What association brought it back—
That memory, so trivial, so satisfactory—
To make these hours of silence, stillness, and confusion
The very nourishment to feed my spirit.

I surrender to every resentment and fear,
Accept the recurrence of hate and envy,
The terrible numbness, the passivity,
As part of myself, as my necessity,
The other half of my mind—no dark, no light,
No past, no future—no past if I can feel that sand
And see those waves, weed, foam, and lift my head
And stare, which I did not do then, towards the horizon.

Rapture

Lead-footed on the ocean's bed
He understood reality.
Intoxication comes with movement.
Recklessness is ecstasy.
Bright weeds and fronds caress
His weightless limbs. Air-bubbles
Rise like beads of mercury,
The visions crowd around,
Pale angel-fish seem friends,
And grottos low in shadowed reefs
Tempt onwards beyond range
Of oxygen or energy.
Something is calling. Delicious
To lay claim to all this realm.
He wrenches off his mask,
Deluded and omnipotent;
Drifts upwards as a suicide.

Sister of Mercy

If she visits those most sick,
Succours the dying,
Can we blame her if
She shows no interest
In any others.

If she needs the reek of death
To feel alive, then
Can we blame her if
The dying love her,
Lift themselves to see her pass
And kiss her hands
With ghastly lips.
They bless her, and she eases
Their last moments—
No doubt of that.
She serves a purpose.

So can we blame her if
She cannot breathe except
Among such exhalations.
Perhaps she once preferred
Fresh air and growing flowers.
Perhaps she knows
Her kindness is suspect
And motives dubious
But cannot find the cruelty
To abdicate the power
The dying grant her,
Nor strength to spurn them.

How can we blame her if
She doubts her doubts
And thus continues.
It will not last too long,
Some day soon she will fall sick.

The Wild Hunt

The hunt is out, torch-light and screams.
The forest shows another face
To those who hide than to pursuers.
Each trunk he glides behind becomes
The axle-tree, and space between—
Spokes of the wheel on which he's bound—
Radiates like avenues.

All animals and birds are hushed.
Focus of the insects' interest,
Their buzz betrays him. Pine-needles
Point, and bushes wilt the better
To expose the alien.
His terror cannot be disguised,
His smell is carried by the wind.

Hunters and undergrowth are intimate.
The wood embraces them so closely
It obscures the quarry.
They crash through thickets, brusquely tear
At vines. Hot shoulders glow
Like rotting fungus—opacity
Of flesh intensified by madness.

The hunt is out. Pack and victim meet.
Sacrifice is made, the forest sated.
God, animal, and human share
The pledge of blood, belief
That through this guilt incorporated
The elements return to balance,
And power renews in every creature.

Hope of Envy

The arrow-head of jealousy
Will fester, being dipped in envy.
But festering is healthy—
Mortification is a form
Of self-defense, the white
Rejection, forces mustered
To eliminate the painful,
Alien fact, the object
Super-real, the throbbing wound.

Envy makes one greedy.
Easier to take than to receive,
Believe the spirit's phagocytes
Efficient to consume
Every infection and intruder
Yet not succumb. The hope of envy
Is release from jealousy,
Recovery from fever, and
Truth's healing slumber.

Neighbour

Too much happens to some people,
Leaves them no time to deepen.

They are completely different
From the established citizen.

Oh, the houses, the journeys,
That have taken my energies.

But then I was younger
And believed myself stronger.

Now I seem to exist
In a torrent of wind

Incurably foreign
As an insect or Martian,

Cannot understand the purpose
Or note more than the surface

Of my neighbour's true quality—
He remains a mystery.

So little happens to some people
And yet they know a secret

Which sustains them, which I cannot
Gain, or long ago forgot.

Sleepers

That was yesterday. Since then
My part of the world slept.
The village lay, horizontal,
Each lapped by his own dream,
Never more unified, more private.
By day, each does his job,
Involved, dependent on others
To use and provide. At night,
Apart, side by side, (if the walls
Should dissolve or fall they'd seem
Cocoons of dreams, mysterious
To an alien observer),
They're linked to other times,
To distant places, stars—
Their sheeted bodies pledges left
As proof the indwelling spirit
Will surely return; dim floats
On the night's black surface
That indicate the exact spot
Where the dreamer sank down
And will rise; to resume his life,
Name, and relationships—
Tomorrow's limitations.

From a Plane

The parquet floor of earth,
Soil worked, enriched,
Seems a stenography
That uses such topography
As rising land and ditch.

Fields seen from high enough above,
Terrace, slope, or plain,
Shift colour, send a signal—
Though men who toil them think
Their only purpose grain.

As those before believed
The shields or sticks they decorated
With patterns now called art
Must be adorned to serve their part
In daily obligation.

But this abstract design,
This picture language,
Implies by its telluric scale
A half-obliterated tale
I guess at hazard.

Dryness

The shale glints sullenly
Exuding mineral,
Each strata raw, revealed:
Track where some beast once dragged
Its oozing and enormous foot
Across ridges of eroded land.

The countryside is sick:
Outcrops of scurfy mica,
Iridescent copper—
Bruises, corrosion, fungus,
Every rot and parasitic growth
That prey on flesh or wood
Evoke the livid colours
Of these bad-lands.

Certain events
Fuse areas of the brain
Into the same sterility.
Compressed emotion carbonises.
Naphtha flares till muffled
By its noxious smoke.

Goat of the wilderness,
Licking at salty grass
Near the horizon,
Guilt's scapegoat,
Rank goat of phosphorus.
The wind too dry
Even for perspiration—

No moisture anywhere
To swab away the burning
Flakes, the sheath of fire.

The cactus sucks,
Somehow survives,
Almost appearing inorganic.
Blunt spines defend its succulence.
Fauna reduced
To scorpions and spiders:
Confusions of a brain
Which apprehends the itch of healing
As pain unbearable,
The apogee of desert's dryness.

Scar-Heart

If his heart is seared already
You can never reach it.
Scar-tissue is not flexible,
Does not react. A heart adorned
With disks of rigid scars,
Moon-ornaments, as slick as oyster-shell,
Mother-of-pearl. The battle lost
Before begun, perhaps before your birth.
That slumbering female guardian
In one so-accurate
Though seeming-clumsy swipe
Of claws, marked him for life.
All else is ineffectual.
Only the old scars ache.
Only those joys of which he was deprived
So long ago can satisfy him now.
You're trapped. You must repeat
Another's pattern, having recognised
Your role; enact the same
Betrayals, strain to compensate
For what you cannot help inflict,
And know the miracle impossible.

Love-Story

No need to seek escape in any war.
The war is here, and those who fight—
What else is it they're fighting for
But freedom for just this?—the suffering
I must record, yet know as shameful.

Anything else would be evasion
Of what I owe, I must fulfil
That duty: I've lost the dignity
Of one who's never been in love,
Involved in love's long struggle.

As stripped and stumbling as a refugee
Abandoning his ruined house,
Reduced to mere survival;
(In thrall to love, such luxuries
As kindness shrivel);
If this be peace, this cruelty,
Why are they dying in the jungle?

It took only moral pressure
No need for grosser torture;
He gave no quarter
She was defenceless.

No need for grosser torture
It took only moral pressure;
He was defenceless
She gave no quarter.

Brandenberg

While the concerto plays I imagine Brandenberg,
Remember the winter I played it over and over—
Water lying in sheets on the saturated land,
Unabsorbed, dull browns of reeds and nostalgia,
Spongy apples speckled with white mould
Tangled in wet grass—when I lay in bed and wept,
Too weak, too lax, for anything but self-pity.
Another baby gone—those long, sterile labours
Of miscarriage. All I could do was change the records,
As fog drifted greyly from the River Mimram
And the Scotch kale corroded to plumboge green
And purple in the frost-burned garden.
Weeds on the road-edge black, rotten, and stiff.
When I went outside they sickened and frightened me.
I closed the windows, shut the door of every room,
Huddled by the kitchen range and sewed, and listened
Through the needle's hissing for some explanation.

The Bull

Tauric, Mithraic, stubborn,
Only blood finally means anything.
How many times already
The bloody tears have flowed, each time
Its source more dangerous and vital;
How long will it be possible
To go on losing blood, to pay
The tithe of energy? Such sacrifice
Becomes less ritual and less
Symbolic, at each repetition.

Through limestone passages the chosen bull
Is led. He stinks with fear.
That smell lingers through centuries.
Forced to his knees, he must be dragged
Between the narrow walls that scrape his sides.
Lamps dazzle his eyes, moss burns on oil—
Or are they distant stars seen from
The pastures where he still is lord?
Even the men are crouching, spines curved
As if already dead, smeared with
Red ochre, weapons and food prepared
For afterlife in deeper caves somewhere.

Blood can renew itself eternally
Blood nourishes the stone
And water eats the stone away
And water calcifies in caves
—The streams the mountains' veins—
The lime-hard water seeps through roots
Through bodies curved like embryos
Within the womb of earth, waiting
To putrify or petrify,
Soul nourished by bull's blood.
And water, till once more it rise.

Along raised paths the soul roams free.
Grass-tufts are powdery with chalk,
Roots twisted into nodes to hold
Pale soil from crumbling. But under-cliff
Is dark, slick with a yellow-ochre
Wetness, though the sea too calm
To reach such height, and no beach shows,
No pebbles to be covered by
A higher tide. The water lifts,
Recedes, yet that clear line
Is not achieved by any surge.

Then water sucks away, as if
A far catastrophe were drawing back
All ocean to its umbilicus.
The sea-bed lies exposed and livid
As body suffering love's urgency;
And graven in that bone-white stone,
As clear as when it first plunged down:
The shape of an enormous bull.

Fruit

Peeling an orange,
Cutting the skin in quarters,
I was overcome
By memory of how
You used to peel my fruit for me.
You loved me. I remember now.

So long ago, though it was only
Yesterday, I vowed
Never to speak again
Of all the past, not even
Open my mouth,
If what I said seemed blame.

Pure misery to know
One is no longer loved.
Hot tears will flow
But offer no relief.
Remorse and grief.
My first test failed.
I could not keep my promise
To myself. I had to speak.
Another wedge is driven in.

So much already said
Where can silence begin?
Not before telling you,
(Though I appreciate its irony),

How as your love has waned
Mine grows, a fruit
With husk so hard
It seemed to need
Such painful fire for ripening.

Progress

The doctor tightens up a bolt.
His monster winces as the screw bites deeper.
It's pain that makes those arms reach out,
Jerks both legs forward clumsily.
'That's progress!' the mad doctor cries in glee.
Almost he does embrace his creature.
The monster's in a swoon of agony,
The circuits now connected generate
Self-loathing. Doc does not know about
Such variation from his blueprints—
It is an error: introspection
Was not included in the plan.
When pressure is relaxed, the monster
Slumps back, useless to his master,
But praising every god of progress.

A Fairy Story

The princess in the fairy story
Discovered that a happy ending
Had unexpected consequences.
The castle in the wood concealed
A certain chamber; her knight revealed
A taste for flagellation; and when
He tired of protests and capitulation,
He rode away—until another kingdom,
Dragon, maiden who could not be won
By any simpler method, was stumbled on.

He then would stay, enter the lists.
He loved the risk, the praise, that combat
Or the guessing game where death
Remained the final forfeit. He loved
A distraught princess, never could resist.
Their fear attracted, their wavering spirit.

Once upon a time, their taming was
The reason for his quest, but now exhaustion,
Boredom, made him pleased his dragon—
Surrogate could test them first.
If they survived the monster's ardent breath
That smoky taint made them delicious.

The rescued princesses compared
Sad stories, boasted of their sufferings,
Exaggerating the ordeal.
They dressed each other's hair, changed
Robes and jewels, waited impatiently
To see the girl who next would join them.

One day, outside the crumbling walls
Of some obscure and unimportant
Principality, the knight was bested.
The dragon fled, dragging bruised coils
Through hedges, across muddy ploughed-land.
The princess would not follow him,
But turned her back and went inside the town.
The watchers were not more nonplussed.

The knight rode home, sent messages
To all his friends. They drank and sang,
Tortured his wives—they had an orgy.
Next day he bade farewell to each
Blood-brother, each noble companion,
Vowed the remaining years to penance
Somewhere far from this vile shambles.

But first, before he set off with his squire
Down that faint narrow path which lured
Deep into the misty forest,
A splendid tomb must be constructed:
Memorial to those princesses—
Obedient victims of his destiny.
The monument still stands, although
The castle fell to ruins long ago.
The knight died on a battle field.
Their legend: fatalistic, gory,
Suitable matter for a fairy story.

Poem

First it's a week, then a month, then a year.
I can tell myself there's nothing to fear—
That even a year is as nothing compared
To the length of a life. But empty time
Augments, has its own demands and rights.
The fear itself becomes my life unless
I leave some mark to prove I was here
Except these scabs I've worried off
The wounds I won't allow to heal—but flaunt,
Preserve, admire, and call it art.

Beardsley's 'St. Rose of Lima'

Levitation's diagram
Charted in lines of black on white.
The jet of energy
Propelling her seems effortless.
Surging drapery covers her feet:
The image Buñuel once used
When son dreams of his mother,
Woman pure, impossible.
Weight of meat bends back her wrists:
Acceptance of whatever comes.
The cotton robe a plinth of folds
Heavy as moulded plaster,
Wet-pack sheet; face an oval blank
Of ecstasy, the meeting point
Of saintliness, carnality.
Saint Rose of Lima smiles
So meltingly, and Jesus
Seems as beautiful as Tristan.

Rites of Passage

My pain should be contained
Within a ritual.
I need to be reborn,
The time has come. I seek
My helpers, midwives of
The spirit, those who went
Before and thus could teach
Me, but I find no-one.

I am not sick, this is
A natural process.
But not since caves were tombs
And shelters, temples where
One dreamt the oracle
On alcove's ledge
Would I be so alone.

I need all strength for birth
But waste that force
In muffling labour-groans.
No chanting voices help
By their distraction, no
Drugging smoke to lull me,
No sacred wine and meat.

I fear to ask, lest I
Be utterly ignored.
Grotesque my pangs have seemed
To those I once approached.
Barbaric now to drag
Myself between the rocks,
Bite through the navel-cord,
And hope the child will live.

Green

Green falls apart into
Its yellow and its blue,
Will not hold together.
Moss and olive leaves,
Opposite hues—
Moss glows solar,
Sun's spectrum at its centre;
Olive, bloomed and secretive,
Opaque as the full moon.

Between blue and yellow
Green fuses into unity.
It signifies untried,
Is hope's pure colour—
Also means envy,
Jealousy, and other
Manifestations of
Life's flowing energy.
Moon oozes blue,
Sun sweats yellow.
Green grows between the two.

Freedom Defined

Freedom cannot be seen against hostility,
    it fades and bleaches out,
      pales to the camouflage of hatred.
Freedom includes delight at recognising
    that there is hardly anything
      to be desired.
Freedom, the great desire consuming every other.
Freedom has no companions or relationships.
Freedom for any purpose becomes limitation.
Freedom from needs is death.
Freedom from love is death.
Freedom from time is immortality—
    the realm of animals and saints
                 —or death.

The White Bird

After great grief, how slowly
Secondary feelings then return.
All daily matters must be learned again
After such strain, such effort.

Uncertain yet if more than life was saved,
Remembrance of bird-song is salvaged.
Perhaps it was a message, but
Survival's concentration deafened.

It might be madness, this conviction.
Crisis engulfs. Surely not one bird
Could last on that mid-ocean rock
When battered by so fierce a tempest.

Hope is a white bird, but fear saw only
Hurtling water mounting upwards,
Green wall blocking land and sky,
The terror of reversed direction.

When storm abates, all drifting wreckage
Must be gathered and examined. While
Waiting for that bird to sing again,
Hope strengthens and adorns her shelter.

The Lambs

The lambs are separated from their mothers.
Bleating is louder than birdsong or engine.
And on the marsh the mother sheep are restive,
The shepherd warns us, for their lost young ones.

The children ask if they will recognise
Each other, later in the year, at pasture
In some green field where they are put together?
I say I doubt it, and both fall silent.

Throughout the night they huddled by the hedges
Moaning, awake—and yet the children slept
As peacefully as lambs should, undisturbed:
My own child, and the one whose mother's dead.

At last the wind drowns out their agitation.
Quiet again, the house seems usual.
Why must I try to make these unrelated facts
Combine into a soothing explanation.

Last Chance, Last Hope

She clung to him like a witch
To her broomstick, like
A soldier to his angel.
She fell into his arms
Like jumping from a burning ship—
Without hesitation—from
A plane spiralling down,
Every control frozen, locked.

She wound her arms around him
Like a woman whom the sea
Has rejected already
Two times, knowing the third
Would be fatal. But he
Will save her. A small smile
On her lips at the memory
Of the waves, the flames, the shock,
The turbulence; nausea
From the drinks and ointments
They applied to her body
Before that launching.
It seems so distant.

He will support her,
Carry her high and away—
Her saviour, source of delight,
Last chance, last hope,
Her instrument of power—
With nothing left to pay
For other miracles
Should this one fail.

Words and Letters

Comic or tragic, prose
Or poetry, I use
The same few letters.
They are my tools, also
The raw material.

I seek the words which will
Define the Word—scoop out
The clay with clay, hack stone
With stone, drill deep for metal.
Each force must meet another
Equal force, the paradox
Where truth confronts a truth
As logical, and yet
Totally dissimilar.

Beneath the words are other
Words, behind the marks
Upon this paper other
Shapes, between the letters
Links which might dissolve
So easily, and then unite
Into quite other words,
Assume a pattern
Just as satisfying.

The letters dance before
My eyes, they dazzle me,
It is a game we share.
But I shall always seek
What they keep hiding—
This game is final.

Grace-Notes

My solemn simplicities, my vows,
My protestations. Tum-te-tum—
Self-accusations. I don't know how
To free myself, to overcome.
Except sometimes, a bird or a tree,
The light on the marsh—direct,
Without equivocation—speak
Of a power that seeks no effect
Outside itself, existing purely,
For which there are no synonyms.
It's a zone I approach unsurely,
That harsh place—where no hymning
Can drown the weak, explaining voice,
Nor grace-notes disguise the wrong choice.

Statement

'Cet animal est très méchant,
Quand on l'attaque il se défend.'

This is the animal I am:
I need what animals
Can never live without,
Food, water, air—
But even more,
A sense of power,
Some territory where
I feel I have significance.
I dream of speech,
A flower between my teeth,
—And long for peace—
Mais on doit s\deféndre.